Chart Symbols

Admiralty Chart 5011 is actually a book showing all the chart symbols. Here, we will just concentrate on some common dangers such as rocks and shallows. You must know these:

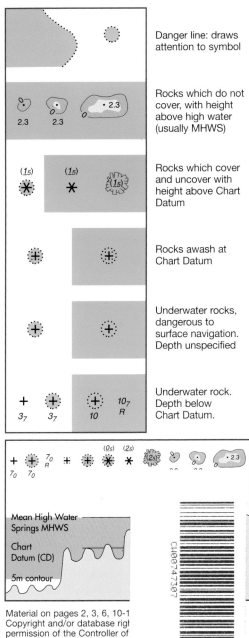

Danger line: draws attention to symbol

Rocks which do not cover, with height above high water (usually MHWS)

Rocks which cover and uncover with height above Chart Datum

Rocks awash at Chart Datum

Underwater rocks, dangerous to surface navigation. Depth unspecified

Underwater rock. Depth below Chart Datum.

Mean High Water Springs MHWS

Chart Datum (CD)

5m contour

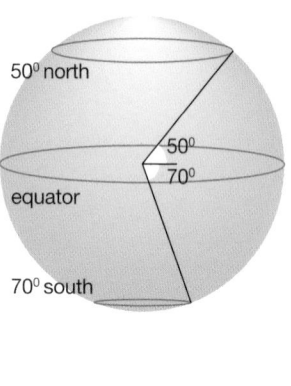

Parallels of latitude

Measured in degrees from equator, eg 50° N or 70° S.
Up to 90°.
1 degree = 60 minutes 1° = 60'
Minutes are then divided into tenths or hundredths, eg 50°37'.62 N.

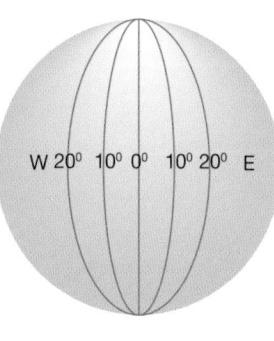

Meridians of longitude

0° goes through Greenwich. E and W measured from there (up to 180°) eg 10° 25'.37 E

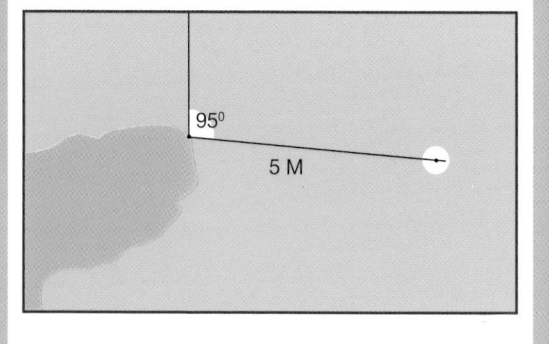

Position

Position is given as lat (first) and long, eg the position of North Foreland Light is 51° 22'.47 N 001° 26'.80 E.
Alternatively, position can be given as a (true) bearing and distance *from* a known point, eg, 095° North Foreland Light 5 miles.

Distance

One nautical mile = 1 minute of latitude
1M = 1' ≈ 1853 metres ≈ 2000 yards
= 10 cables ≈ 1.15 statute miles

Note: Speed is measured in knots
1 knot = 1 nautical mile per hour = 1.136 mph.

Finding the Latitude and Longitude of a Point on the Chart

1 To find the latitude, use the dividers to measure from a horizontal line to the point. 2 Now move the open dividers to the latitude scale, align to the horizontal line and read off the latitude (here, it is 50° 16.3'N).

3 & 4 Find the longitude in a similar way. (Here, it is 3° 57.7'W.)

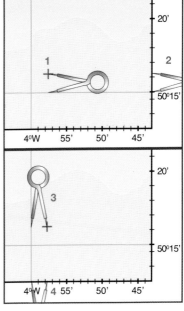

Transfering a Latitude and Longitude to the Chart

A To transfer 50° 16.3'N 3° 57.7'W, first open the dividers like this. B Move the dividers to roughly the correct latitude and draw a line like this _____.

C Now set the dividers for the longitude.

D Transfer to the line already drawn and mark the longitude ——|——. The intersection is 50° 16.3'N 3° 57.7'W.

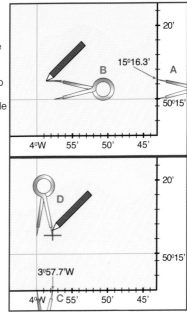

The Compass Variation

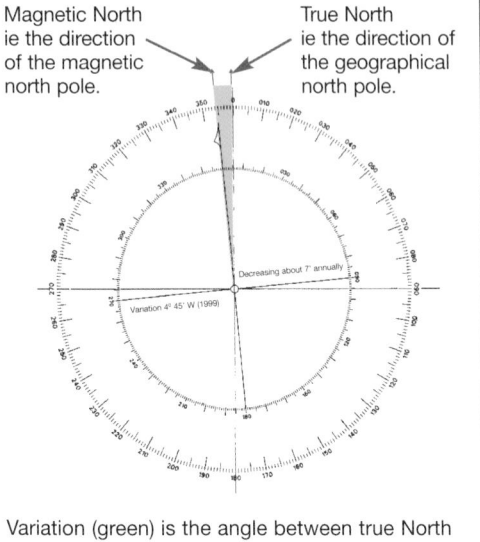

Magnetic North ie the direction of the magnetic north pole.

True North ie the direction of the geographical north pole.

Decreasing about 7' annually

Variation 4° 45' W (1999)

Variation (green) is the angle between true North and magnetic North. It changes with position and time. On this chart it is 4° 45' W in 1999.
In 2009 it will be about 3° 35' W.

Deviation

Theoretically the needle in a magnetic compass points to magnetic North, but the compass in most boats is subject to magnetic interference from the engine, the electrics and electronics.

Any error caused is known as deviation.

- Deviation is the angle between a magnetic bearing and the same bearing taken by a particular compass in a particular boat.
- Unlike variation, deviation varies according to the boat's heading. To see why this is, imagine that all the 'interference' in a boat behaves as though it is concentrated into a fixed iron block.

Compass should point here.

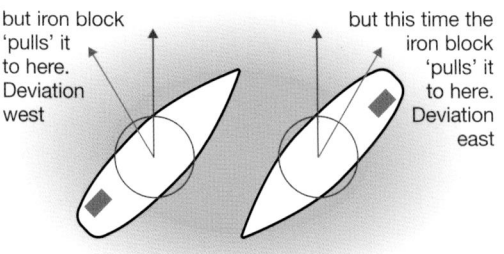

but iron block 'pulls' it to here. Deviation west

but this time the iron block 'pulls' it to here. Deviation east

In practice deviation is often reduced to a minimum or removed altogether by a compass adjuster. He will swing the compass to find out the deviation on various headings, then place magnets to remove or reduce it. He will then produce a Deviation Table for you.

Converting Bearings

1 For the order of converting types of bearing simply remember the mnemonic:
True **V**irgins **M**ake **D**ull **C**ompanions.

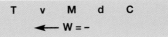

2 Error West, Compass Best, ie compass reads bigger.

T	v	M	d	C
		← W = −		

If going to the left along the row, subtract westerly deviation or variation. Add easterly deviation or variation. If going to the right, add westerly error. Subtract easterly error.

Example: Compass gives bearing 090°. Deviation 4° W. Variation 3° W. What is True bearing?

T	v	M	d	C
083	-3	086	-4	090

Answer 083° T

If the boat points true North, compass needle will align along X. A bearing of 090° Compass will be Y. From True North this is 083° (T).

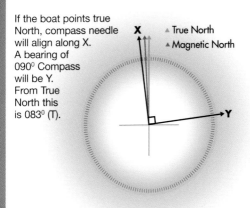

- X
- ▲ True North
- ▲ Magnetic North
- → Y

Example: True bearing 130°. Variation 5 degrees W. Deviation 3° E. What is Compass bearing?

T	v	M	d	C
W −	←	→ W +		
130°(T)	+5	=135°(M)	-3	= 132°(C)

Error is the sum of Variation and Deviation.

With a handbearing compass, cautiously assume deviation is zero. Check by continuously taking a bearing with the handbearing compass on a distant object, while turning the boat through 360°.

Rise and Fall of the Tide

- In most areas there is a High Water and a Low Water every 12 hours 20 minutes.

- The size of the rise and fall varies from area to area: it might be 12 m in the Bristol Channel, 4 m off Harwich.

- **Spring tides** (springs) occur when the sun and moon are in line, relative to the earth. This happens two days after new and full moon. At springs the high tides are higher and the low tides are lower. Highest spring tides occur around 21 March and 23 September at the Vernal and Autumn Equinoxes.

- **Neap tides** (neaps) occur when sun and moon are offset, midway between full and new moon. The rise and fall is smallest.

- **Range of the tide** is the difference in height between successive high and low waters.

- **Chart datum** (CD) is the level to which soundings and drying heights on a chart are referred. In practice it is the lowest height to which the tide is ever expected to fall.

- **Charted depth** is the actual sounding shown on a chart, being the depth of the sea bed below chart datum, and the least depth expected to occur in that place under normal conditions.

- **Actual depth** - at any time, is what it says, and is the charted depth plus the height of the tide, as obtained from Tide Tables.

- **Drying height** is the height above chart datum of any feature that is occasionally covered.

- **Duration** (of the tide) - the time between HW and the previous LW.

- **Mean High Water Springs** (MHWS) - the average height of all the spring highs.

- **Mean Low Water Springs** (MLWS) - the average height of all the spring lows.

- **Mean High Water Neaps** (MHWN) - the average height of all the neap highs.

- **Mean Low Water Neaps** (MLWN) - the average height of all the neap lows.

Tide Tables

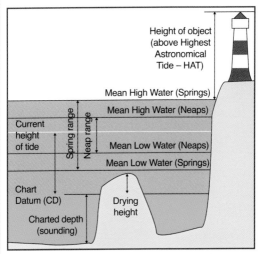

In almanacs and Admiralty tide tables, times and heights of HW and LW are given for each day for a number of large ports known as Standard Ports. Other smaller ports and harbours are listed as Secondary Ports (see page 12).

Local tide tables are available for many individual ports.

Tide tables are in this form, and are given in UT for British waters.

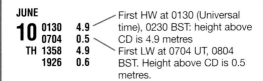

JUNE

10	0130	4.9
	0704	0.5
TH	1358	4.9
	1926	0.6

First HW at 0130 (Universal time), 0230 BST: height above CD is 4.9 metres

First LW at 0704 UT, 0804 BST. Height above CD is 0.5 metres.

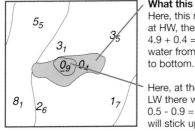

What this means
Here, this morning at HW, there will be 4.9 + 0.4 = 5.3 m of water from surface to bottom.

Here, at the first LW there will be 0.5 - 0.9 = -0.4, ie land will stick up 0.4 m!

The times given in tide tables for UK ports will be in Universal Time (UT). During BST add one hour to times in the table. Tables for continental ports will show local standard time and will give a correction to adjust to UT. Boats cruising near a continental port may, of course, be using local time.

Tide tables give times and heights of HW and LW for a standard port. Intermediate heights and times are deduced from the accompanying curve.

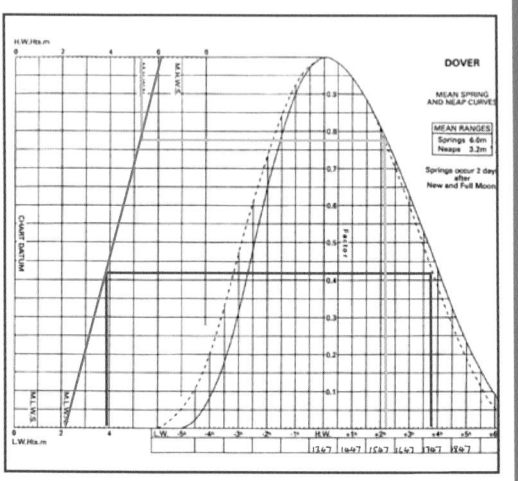

FEBRUARY

	Time	m
16	0136	6.4
	0852	1.1
M	1347	6.1
	2100	1.2

Range is 5.3.
Nearer springs

Required: the height of the tide at Dover at 1557

1 On the Dover tidal diagram plot heights of HW and LW each side of the required time and join them up with a sloping line (red).
2 Enter the HW time and other times as necessary in the boxes below the curves.
3 From the required time 1557 draw a line vertically to the curve (green). The range on the day concerned is nearer the Spring range and therefore the Spring curve (solid line) is used.
4 Proceed horizontally to the red sloping line and hence vertically to the height scale to read 5.1 m.

Required: the time at which the afternoon height of the tide falls to 3.5 m

1 Plot in the times of HW and LW and join them with a sloping line (red) as before.
2 Enter HW time and others to cover the required event.
3 From the required height (3.5 m) proceed vertically (blue) to the sloping line (red) and then across to the spring curve. Dropping down to the time scale, required time is 1737.

The 'Rule of Twelfths'

This gives a useful approximation of intermediate heights, it assumes the tidal curve is 'perfect'. Of course it should not be used where the tide is irregular.

Assuming about six hours between high and low water, this rule says that the rise and fall of the tide is:

1/12 of range in 1st hour	2/12 of range in 2nd hour
3/12 of range in 3rd hour	3/12 of range in 4th hour
2/12 of range in 5th hour	1/12 of range in 6th hour

(1,2,3 - 3,2,1)

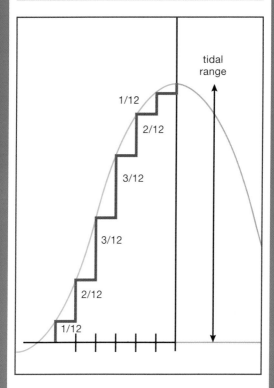

Example:

Here is the tide table for Port X. How much will the tide have fallen 2 hours after the first HW?

JUNE

10 0130   4.9 > 4.4m
    0704   0.5
TH 1358   4.9
    1926   0.6

Tidal range is 4.4m.
In 2 hours tide will have fallen about
1/12 + 2/12 of range = **1.1 metres**

For each Secondary Port there are a set of corrections (known as 'differences') to be applied to the figures for the relative Standard Port. For example: Penzance

Standard Port DEVONPORT (—►)

Times				Height (metres)			
High Water		Low Water		MHWS	MHWN	MLWN	MLWS
0000	0600	0000	0600	5·5	4·4	2·2	0·8
1200	1800	1200	1800				
Differences PENZANCE							
–0055	–0115	–0035	–0035	+0·1	0·0	–0·2	0·0

It helps to remember that the left hand side deals with the time differences and the right side with heights - two separate issues. Note this table is in Universal Time.

These corrections are irregular. For instance, in the example above, if the time of HW Devonport is around 0000 or 1200, the correction to be applied for Penzance is -55 min. But if the Devonport HW is around 0600 or 1800, then the correction is -75 min (1 hr 15 min). In this particular case there is no variation in the differences for LW.

Similarly, when the height of HW Devonport is 5.5 m, HW at Penzance will be 0.1 m higher. When the height at Devonport is 4.4 m, HW at Penzance will be no higher.

Clearly there are times when interpolation is needed. For instance, in the figures above there is a 20 minute difference between the corrections for a 1200 HW and an 1800 HW. So, interpolating 'by eye', the correction for a HW around 1500 would be -65 minutes.

Interpolation can be carried out graphically as the following two examples show.

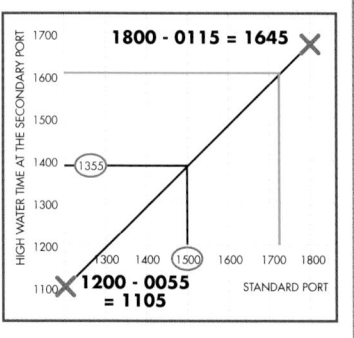

What is the time of HW Penzance when HW Devonport is 1500 UT?

HW Penzance is 1355 UT

Remember: work in UT and convert to BST at the end, if necessary.

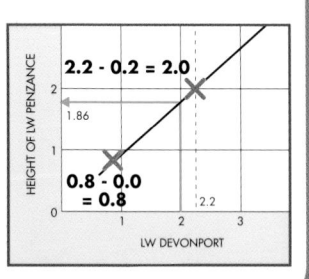

When LW Devonport is 2.0 m what is LW Penzance?

1.86 m = 1.9 m

Intermediate Times and Heights

The procedure for calculating the height of the tide at secondary ports at intermediate times between HW and LW is essentially the same as for standard ports. There are no tidal curves for secondary ports, so the curve for the appropriate standard port is used. We 'pretend' this is the curve for the secondary port, and put onto it the secondary port's times and heights.

What is the height of tide at 1300 BST at Penzance?

Use the example of Penzance on the previous page when the tide table for Devonport shows:

7	0348	4.7
	0955	1.4
TU	1614	4.9
	2221	1.4

HW Devonport = 1614 UT = 1714 BST
From table on previous page HW Penzance = 1604 BST (green line).

Use the Devonport curve as a 'pretend' Penzance curve, and mark in this time of HW.
HW Devonport = 4.9
and interpolating **HW Penzance** is 4.9 (4.9-0.0)
LW Devonport is 1.4
and interpolating **LW Penzance** is 1.3 (1.4-0.1)
Add these to the 'Penzance' curve.
Read off the height of tide at 1300 as previously:

Answer 3.6 m.

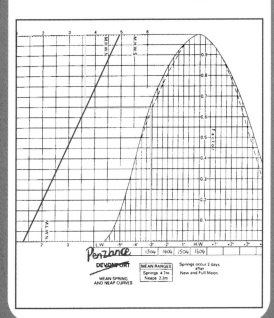

Definitions

Tidal streams are the horizontal movement of the water caused by the vertical rise and fall. If the tide drops in a harbour, then the water has to flow somewhere! The stream normally changes direction about every six hours, although the change is not necessarily at local HW or LW.

Set (expressed in three figures - eg 160 degrees) is the direction in which a tidal stream flows measured in degrees True. Note: The wind's direction is FROM where it blows. A tidal set indicates the direction the stream flows TOWARDS.

Rate (in knots) is the speed at which a tidal stream flows.

Drift is the distance the stream carries in a period of time.

A tide race occurs where a strong tidal stream passes through a narrow passage, or off a headland. Dangerous, especially if wind against tide.

Overfalls are caused by tide flowing strongly over an uneven seabed.

Tidal Stream Information

Tidal stream charts
- Very useful for passage planning
- Come in sets of 12 (Almanacs or Tidal Stream Atlases)
- Arrows indicate direction of stream (degrees T)
- Length and thickness of arrow indicates strength
- Rate indicated by figures, eg 04,08 means 0.4 knots neaps, 0.8 knots springs
- Comma indicates position data was recorded
- Interpolate if between springs and neaps

Example:
What is the tidal stream off Dundee 2 hours after HW Dover?

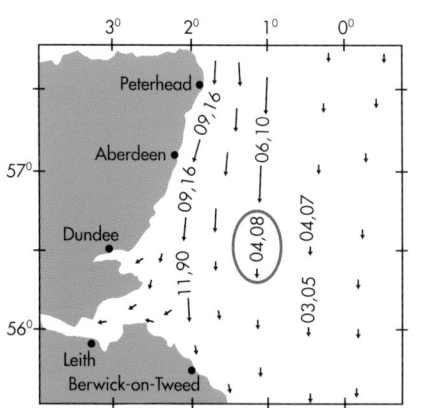

7

0359	1.5
0918	5.9
1627	1.5
2135	6.0

Range is 4.4 m. Draw AB on the Computation of Rates table. From 4.4 draw CD. DE gives the interpolation, 0.5 knots.

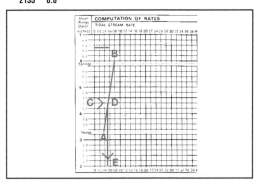

The information from tidal diamonds is more detailed than the atlases, but may be very localised.

- Very useful for course to steer and course made good.
- Position of ◇ will be shown on the chart. Lat and Long are also given.

Take 2 hrs before HW Dover as an example. From 2.5 hours to 1.5 hours before HW the stream runs at 218° T. At springs it runs at 1.0 knots, at neaps 0.5 knots. Interpolate between springs/neaps, depending on range at Portsmouth (see green lines below). Tidal stream is 0.9 knots.

10

0627	1.0	range
1121	6.5	5.5
F 1848	1.0	
2337	6.5	

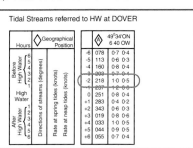

Tidal Streams referred to HW at DOVER

Hours	◇ Geographical Position	◇ 49°34'ON 6 40 OW
	Directions of streams (degrees)	Rate at spring tides (knots) / Rate at neap tides (knots)
Before High Water 6 5 4 3 2 1	-6 078	0·7 0·4
	-5 113	0·6 0·3
	-4 160	0·8 0·4
	-3 003	0·7 0·4
	-2 218	1·0 0·5
	-1 237	1·2 0·6
High Water	0 251	0·8 0·4
After High Water 1 2 3 4 5 6	+1 283	0·4 0·2
	+2 343	0·6 0·3
	+3 019	0·8 0·6
	+4 033	1·0 0·5
	+5 044	0·9 0·5
	+6 055	0·7 0·4

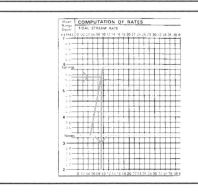

How to Obtain Tidal Set (Direction) and Drift (Distance) Over a Period

Example. Find the set and drift near ◈ from 1100 to 12.30 on 23 August.

- Find the nearest tidal diamond (in this case ◈) or tide arrow.

Tidal Streams referred to HW at DOVER

Hours	◇ Geographical Position			◇ 49°34'ON 6 40 OW	
		Directions of streams (degrees)	Rate at spring tides (knots)	Rate at neap tides (knots)	
Before High Water 6				078	0·7 0·4
5				113	0·6 0·3
4				160	0·8 0·4
3				203	0·7 0·4
2				218	1·0 0·5
High Water 1				237	1·2 0·6
0				251	0·8 0·4
After High Water 1				283	0·4 0·2
2				343	0·6 0·3
3				019	0·8 0·6
4				033	1·0 0·5
5				044	0·9 0·5
6				055	0·7 0·4

- Look up the relevant tide tables (Dover, in this case)

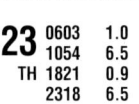

23	0603	1.0
	1054	6.5
TH	1821	0.9
	2318	6.5

HW Today = 1054 UT + 1 hr
= 1154 BST Range Dover = 5.5 m

- Make a Tidal Set and Drift Table (below). Enter time of HW (11.54). Tide is given for half an hour before to half an hour after this (11.24 to 1224). Mark up rest of times.
- Our period includes half an hour at the HW-1 rate, and one hour at the HW rate.
- Interpolate between Springs and Neaps.

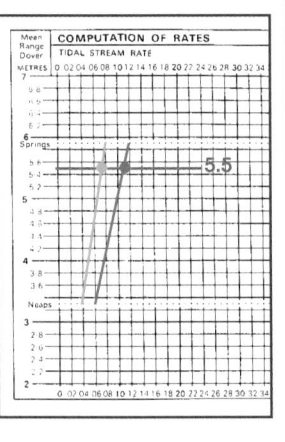

So the tidal effect in 1¹⁄₂ hours is:

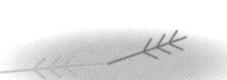

TIDAL SET and DRIFT TABLE

TIME		◇	SET	RATES			DURN.	DIST
				SPRINGS	NEAPS	INTERPLN		
BEFORE HW	-6 to -2							
	1024	A	237°T	1·2	0·6	1·1	½	0·55
HIGH WATER 1154	1124	A	251°T	0·8	0·4	0·7	1 hr.	0·7
	1224							
AFTER HW	+2 to +6							

1. Insert HIGH WATER times
2. Add/subtract 30 mins to give start and end of HW bap.
3. Complete TIME column.
4. Insert appropriate DIAMOND, SET and RATE
5. Interpolate RATES if necessary
6. Compute duration of RATE if less than one hour
7. Calculate length of drift (rate x duration).

Dead Reckoning

Dead Reckoning (DR) is plotting a position based on the course steered and distance travelled in a given time.

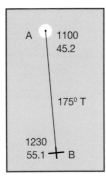

Position at 1100 was A. Log reads 45.2
Course of 175⁰ T was steered until 1230 when log reading was 55.1.
Hence a distance of 9.9 M has been travelled in the direction 175⁰ T and the DR position at 1230 is B.

Dead reckoning makes no allowance for the effects of wind or tide, and thus may be only a theoretical position. But it is still an important part of basic navigation, and far better than having no plot.

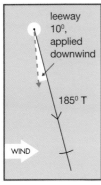

Leeway is the sideways effect of the wind on a boat under sail.The boat is pushed sideways downwind so that its water track is different from the course actually steered.

The effect of leeway depends on varying factors including hull design. It will be felt most when a boat is going to windward and heeled over, less with a beam wind and nil with the wind astern. Leeway is also affected by wind strength and boatspeed and is greatest at slow speed in strong winds.

Leeway can be assessed by looking aft and estimating the difference between the wake and the fore and aft line. But in strong winds, when leeway is likely to be greatest, the sea may be rough and the wake hard to see.

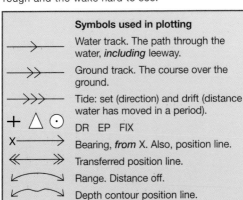

Symbols used in plotting

Water track. The path through the water, *including* leeway.

Ground track. The course over the ground.

Tide: set (direction) and drift (distance water has moved in a period).

DR EP FIX

Bearing, *from* X. Also, position line.

Transferred position line.

Range. Distance off.

Depth contour position line.

18 Estimated Position (EP)

The DR can be inaccurate because it does not allow for leeway or tide. The Estimated Position (EP) does allow for them.

1. Draw your course line AB (any length).
2. Apply leeway and draw the water track AC (any length, provided longer than will be used).
3. Measure off the distance run, AD.
4. Apply the tidal effect from D, to give the EP at E.
5. Draw the ground track AE.

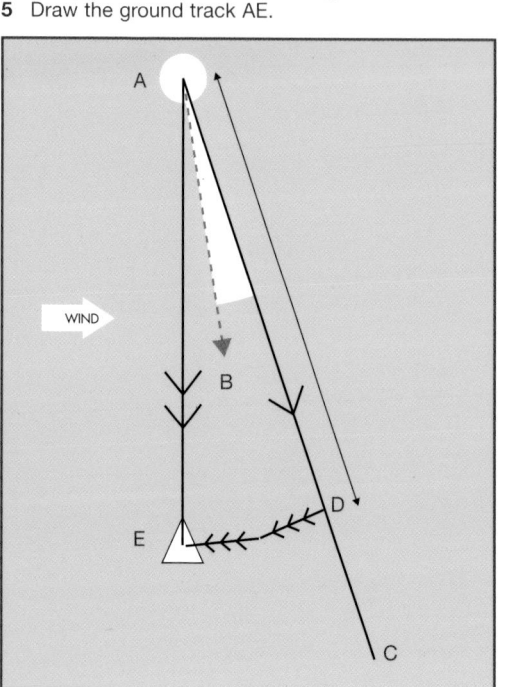

Notes
- When plotting an EP, apply leeway first.
- You actually move along the line AE.

Example

Time	Course steered	Log	Estimated Leeway	Comments
1100	100°T	5.3	10° North	Fix
1200	100°T	10.3	10° North	Work up an EP

We are near Tidal Diamond A

Tidal Streams referred to HW at DOVER

Hours	Directions of streams (degrees)	Rate at spring tides (knots)	Rate at neap tides (knots)		49°34'ON 6 40 OW	
Before High Water 6 5 4 3 2 1				-6	078	0·7 0·4
				-5	113	0·6 0·3
				-4	160	0·8 0·4
				-3	203	0·7 0·4
				-2	218	1·0 0·5
				-1	237	1·2 0·6
High Water				0	251	0·8 0·4
After High Water 1 2 3 4 5 6				+1	283	0·4 0·2
				+2	343	0·6 0·3
				+3	019	0·8 0·6
				+4	033	1·0 0·5
				+5	044	0·9 0·5
				+6	055	0·7 0·4

	23	**0603**	**1.0**
The tide table for (in this case) Dover is:		**1130**	**6.5**
	TH	**1750**	**0.9**
		2359	**6.6**

1 Course line 100°T.

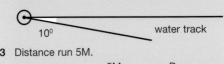

WIND

2 Leeway 10°. Draw the water track.

10°   water track

3 Distance run 5M.

5M   D

4 Work out the tidal effect.
High Water today = 11.30 UT + 1 hour = 12.30 BST
Range Dover = 6.5 - 1.0 = 5.5m
At 11.30 (the mid-point of our hour) we are at HW -1.The tide runs at 237°T 1.2 kn springs, 0.6 kn neaps

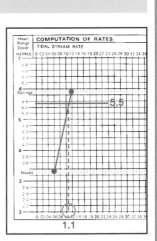

COMPUTATION OF RATES

5.5

1.1

From computation of Rates Table it runs at 1.1 kn today. So, from 1100 to 1200 the tide takes us 1.1 mile in direction 237°T.

Apply this from position D to give the EP.

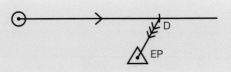

D

EP

5 Draw the ground track.

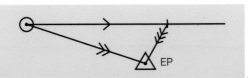

EP

19 Estimated Position (EP)

Allowing for the Tide

Clearly it is better to plot a course that compensates for the wind and tide and lets you 'make good' your required course.

Example:

Starting from point A at 1100 it is required to make good a course of 175° to reach point B. Boatspeed is estimated at 5 knots, and tidal stream is the same as that shown on page 16. Westerly wind, leeway 10°.

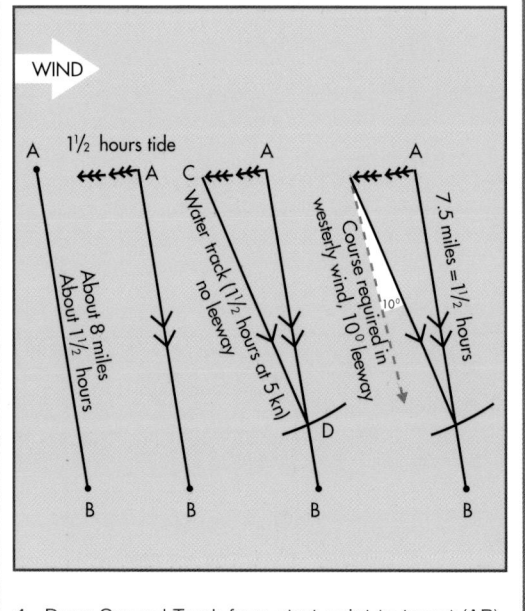

1 Draw Ground Track from start point to target (AB) and beyond. Measure the distance approximately.
2 Anticipate average achievable speed and determine likely passage time (5 knots, about 1.5 hours).
3 Extract, interpolate and construct the tidal vectors (set and drift) from A.
4 From C arc off the distance vector (average speed x anticipated time). This meets AB at D.
5 Join up this arc mark to the end of tide vector – this is the WATER TRACK CD.
6 Length along Ground Track to the arc mark is the Distance Made Good (AD).
7 Calculate Speed Made Good by dividing this by anticipated time (see Point 2): AD/1.5.
8 Work out ETA from $\dfrac{\text{Dist to go}}{\text{Speed Made Good}}$ + start time
9 Add or subtract leeway to "oppose" the wind.
10 Convert Water Track from degrees (T) to degrees (C) to give Course to Steer.

Note:

Plotting a Course to Steer, apply leeway at the end.

Identifying Lights

Lights are shown on the chart like this:

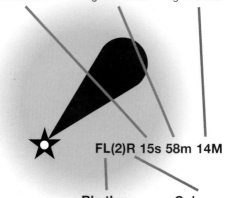

Period:
(here, 2 flashes plus darkness repeated every 15 seconds

Elevation:
The height of the light above MHWS, eg. 58 metres

Range:
Distance light can be seen in normal visibility, eg 14 miles

FL(2)R 15s 58m 14M

Rhythm:

 FL Flashing

 F Fixed

eg FL(2) Group flashing

 Oc Occulting

Iso Isophase: equal periods of light and dark

Q Quick

VQ Very Quick

Colour:
(white if no colour shown)
R = Red
G = Green
Y = Yellow

Sectored Lights

Example:
Light flashes every 30 seconds, showing white in some sectors, red in others. Two ranges given, because white shines further than red.

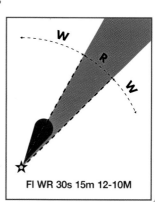

Fl WR 30s 15m 12-10M

Waypoint Navigation

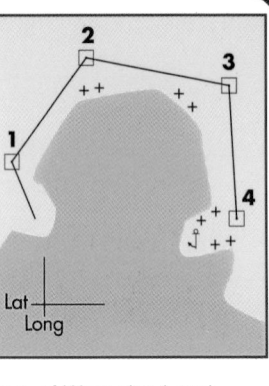

- A waypoint is a point you want to pass through on the way to your destination. A set of these defines the passage - make sure the route between them avoids all dangers.

- Record the lat. and long. of Waypoint 1 and enter in the GPS, not forgetting North/South and East/West eg 50^0 41'.37 N 002^0 30'.29 W
- Label it WP1, and note it in the log.
- Repeat for WP2, WP3, WP4.
- When you set out, the GPS will give a range and bearing (in degrees True or Magnetic - your choice) to WP1.
- Convert to degrees Compass and set off for WP1.
- Use the cross-track function to check your progress. This records your position when the function is switched on and 'draws' a line from it to WP1. It then shows your distance off

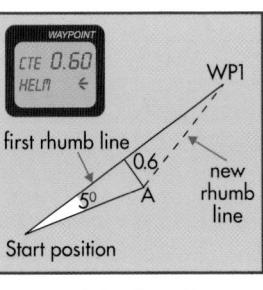

the direct line. eg at A we are 0.6 miles off course, and should turn left.
- Suppose you drift off course (to A), the quickest route from A to WP1 is to plot A, work out the new course to steer but increase the offset (to port). Start the cross track again. This time you should sail straight down the rhumb line, fine-tuning the offset so you do. (This assumes there are no hazards on the new course. Otherwise, turn hard left and go back to the original rhumb line.)

Course Over the Ground (COG) and Speed Over the Ground (SOG)
The GPS gives your COG (True or Magnetic - your choice) and SOG. Comparing this with the compass and speedo gives a measure of the tide and leeway.

Man Overboard Function
Press the MOB button. The GPS enters this as a waypoint and will give you the lat. and long. plus the range and bearing back to the position. Note that the victim will drift away from this position.